A Field Guide to Irish Fairies

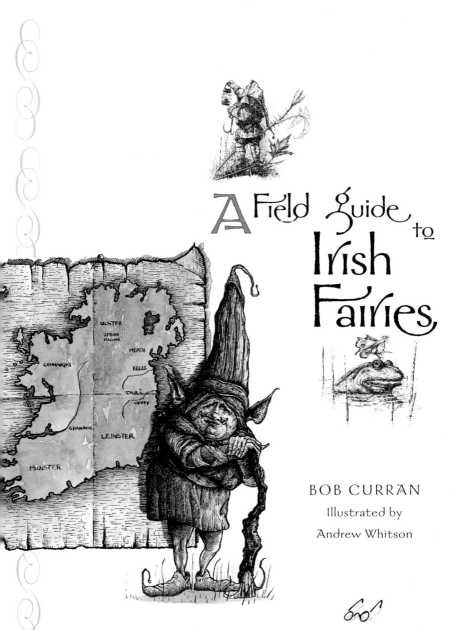

A Field Guide to Irish Fairies

BOB CURRAN

Illustrated by

Andrew Whitson

CHRONICLE BOOKS
SAN FRANCISCO

First published in the United States in
1998 by Chronicle Books.
Copyright © 1997 by Appletree Press.
All rights reserved. No part of this
book may be reproduced in any form
without written permission from
Chronicle Books.

Printed in China

ISBN 0-8118-2276-1

Library of Congress Cataloging-in-
Publication Data available.

Distributed in Canada by
Raincoast Books
8680 Cambie Street
Vancouver, British Columbia V6P 6M9

10 9 8 7 6 5 4 3 2 1

Chronicle Books
85 Second Street
San Francisco, California 94105

www.chroniclebooks.com

Contents

Introduction		Page	8
1	The Grogoch	Page	13
2	The Grey Man	Page	19
3	The Sheerie	Page	25
4	Changelings	Page	31
5	The Pooka	Page	37
6	Merrows	Page	43
7	The Banshee	Page	49
8	The Leprechaun	Page	55
9	The Dullahan	Page	61
Some Lesser Known Irish Fairies		Page	67

Introduction

Fairies have always played a major role in Irish life, and different types of fairy are to be found throughout the Irish countryside. They were once so feared that it was even forbidden to use the word 'fairy' at all, and a number of other, more flattering terms were used to refer to them, such as the Gentry and the Good People.

Who are the fairies and why are they so feared? According to the *Book of Armagh*, they are the old gods of the earth, ancient beings who were once widely worshipped throughout pagan Ireland and who have all but been consigned to memory but who can still make their presence felt when the mood takes them.

Other sources claim that they are fallen angels, those who sat on the fence during the great rebellion in Heaven and who were thrown out for their indecisiveness. They were not, however, consigned to Hell with Lucifer and his followers, being neither good enough to be saved or bad enough to be lost. According to this theory, St Michael (the patron saint of all fairies) interceded with God on their behalf and they were given the dark and remote places of the earth in which to dwell, well away from human habitation. Some were granted the depths of the oceans and became merfolk; others were sent to the lands under the earth and became goblins and trolls; others were granted the air and became spirits and sheeries; whilst others were given the harsh and barren areas of the countryside and became leprechauns and grogochs.

Yet another theory claims that they are the last survivors of the prehistoric race, the Tuatha de Danaan, who came to Ireland from ancient Greece and brought with them skills and magic far in advance of their particular Age. At one time, they were treated as gods but gradually, as Christianity spread across Ireland, they retreated into caves, lonely glens and the hollows which characterise the Irish countryside, venturing out only occasionally.

Fairies can be wilful and capricious creatures, easily offended and quick to anger. They are often spiteful and jealous of mankind, which enjoys a special relationship with God which they cannot. Nevertheless, they can also be good-hearted and merry and many accounts assert the beauty of their music and their love of sport and revelry.

This book attempts to identify those fairies which the reader is most likely to encounter, to detail their origins and characteristics and, where appropriate, to list some of the protections which may be taken against their spiteful ways. It is not, of course, an exhaustive guide, and deliberately so, because I am reminded of a warning given to the Irish poet W B Yeats by the Queen of Fairies, through a Dublin medium. When pressed about the fairies, she simply wrote the following on a piece of paper: "Be careful, and do not seek to know too much about us!"

The grogoch is well-known
throughout north Antrim,
Rathlin Island and
parts of Donegal.

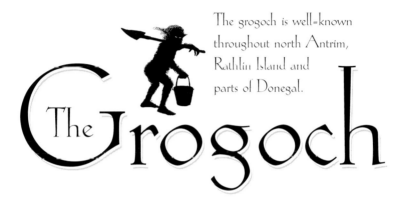

The Grogoch

Variants:
grogock
grigock
gru-og-ock
pecht

An alternative name is 'pecht', a
corruption of Pict, a Celtic race which
once inhabited parts of Scotland. It is
now generally accepted that grogochs
were originally half-human, half-fairy
aborigines who came from Kintyre in
Scotland to settle in Ireland.
Grogochs are also to be found
on the Isle of Man, where they are
called 'phynnodderee'.

13

The Grogoch

The late Robert McCormack, a well known storyteller on Rathlin Island has stated:

"It's fact that the grigocks came from Scotland. They were chased out by the Celtic people who came to live there long ago. They crossed over by a bridge of land that lay between Kintyre and north Antrim. That's why you get so many of them all along the coast and in the islands."

Indeed, the grogoch has parallels throughout the western isles of Scotland, notably on Cara, off the coast of Gigha, and Colonsay, where these fairies are known as 'brownies'.

In appearance, the grogoch resembles an elderly human man; there are no records of any female grogochs. He is about the height of a small child, and completely naked, but covered in coarse, reddish hair or fur. This pelt is thick, dirty, matted and interwoven with twigs and dirt which the grogoch has picked up on his travels: grogochs are not noted for their personal hygiene.

He is wholly benevolent, unlike certain other fairies which he resembles. Most notable of these are the *laughremen*, fairies found only in south Armagh, who are surly and have an unsociable disposition. The laughremen guard hoards of hidden gold and their sole purpose is to drive away inquisitive strangers. The grogoch, however, is genial, good natured and not given to pranks. Although extremely industrious, he is as poor as a church mouse.

The Grogoch

His unkempt appearance has given rise to a number of common expressions along the Antrim coastline. Untidy children around Waterfoot, especially those with unruly hair, are told that they "look like an oul' grogoch" and a dirty house may be said to resemble "the grogoch's midden".

The grogoch's home reflects his hardiness. It is usually in the form of a cave, hollow or cleft in the landscape. In numerous parts of the northern countryside are large 'leaning stones', two standing stones leaning together, which are known as grogochs' houses.

Frank Craig, another Rathlin Island inhabitant, recounts the following: "The grogoch's house is two big stones up near Leg-an-thass-nee. Long ago, if you had been up there, you would have seen them taking their ease of an evening, sitting out in the sun, smoking on Scotch pipes. It's a true thing for I know people, living yet, who seen them".

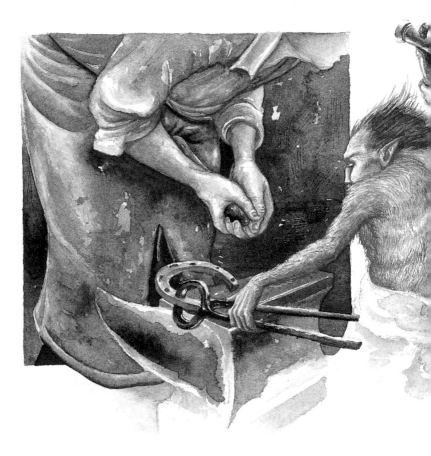

Of all the Irish fairies, the grogoch is perhaps the most sociable towards humans. He may even attach himself to certain individuals and help them with their planting and harvesting or with domestic chores. In this respect, he can be helpful to the point of becoming a nuisance.

His haunt is mainly outdoors and his constitution immune to the extremes of weather – impervious to searing heat or freezing cold. He can survive for long periods without either sleep or food. A workaholic, he may be seen at all times of the day or night, labouring in the fields or fetching and carrying for his neighbours. However, along with many other fairies, he also has the power of invisibility and will often only allow certain trusted people to observe him.

He will scuttle about the kitchen looking for odd jobs to do and will invariably get under the feet of the woman as she goes about her work. For instance, a Rathlin Island woman was bringing a kettle of boiling water from the fire to the table when the grogoch, who had been running around her legs looking for something to do, tripped her and she spilled a drop of boiling water on a sensitive area of his skin. He let out a screech, crying, "Oh! Oh! My viggerald-vaggerald is all scalded!" and fled from the house. Nothing would entice him indoors after that, although he hung around the farmyard, getting in the way of the farmer.

Above all, the grogoch is a tireless worker and cannot tolerate human laziness. He will rouse people who sleep late on a Sunday morning by jumping on their bed and beating them about the face. Likewise, workers taking a break in the hayfields will be continually poked and prodded by the grogoch until they resume work.

This fairy will labour for no payment and to offer him even a small present is to drive him away forever. He will leave with many tears, for he is kind at heart. A jug of cream – the first drawn from the milk – is the only recompense he will accept, drinking it down in one gulp and wiping his whiskers afterwards.

Like many other fairies, the grogoch has a great fear of the clergy and will not enter a house if a priest or minister is there. If the grogoch is becoming a nuisance, it is advisable to get a clergyman into the house and drive the creature away to inadvertently torment someone else.

No other being in the Irish fairy
world is more mysterious or
sinister than the Grey Man.

The Grey Man

Variants:
far liath
an fir lea
brolaghan
Old Boneless

The origins of the Grey Man are
uncertain, but he is known by a variety
of names. In the more westerly parts
of Ireland, in Galway, Sligo and Kerry,
he is known by the anglicised name of
Old Boneless.

The Grey Man

This fairy often appears as a thick and clinging fog, which covers both land and sea with a wet mantle. And although he inhabits mainly coastal areas, he may also be found on high ground and in deep, boggy hollows.

In north Antrim, he is known as the *brolaghan* (from the Irish, meaning a formless or shapeless thing). The latter nomenclature is not strictly accurate, for brolaghans are themselves a specific type of fairy with no particular type of affinity with either mist or fog. It is likely that the Grey Man is the fairy form of an old Celtic weather or storm god, *an fir lea*, who was worshipped by coastal communities around 1500 BC.

So mysterious is this fairy that several conflicting physical descriptions exist. In Waterford and Wexford, he is regarded as little more than a hazy and ragged shadow, moving against the sun and trailing mist in his wake. In Kerry and Clare, he is a being of man-size proportions wrapped in a grey cloak made out of wreathing fog which he continually swirls about him. In Antrim and Down, he is a cloudy, cowled giant, robed like a monk in misty garments and glimpsed far out at sea or above distant mountains.

Being a creature of mist and fog, the Grey Man sustains himself on the smoke from the chimneys of houses. For this reason, he is one of the few fairies that will venture close to large towns or cities, where he can be just as troublesome as in the country or the scattered communities along the seashore. You know when he passes, for his cloak smells musty and unpleasant, heavy with the smell of woodsmoke and peat, and he leaves a cold, clammy air in his wake.

The Grey Man delights in the loss of human life and may use his misty cloak to deadly effect. For example, he may obscure rocks along a coast so that passing ships will smash into them; or he may obscure a road so that a traveller becomes lost or plunges to his death over a dangerous precipice.

Nor are you safe from the Grey Man's attentions if you remain indoors. His touch turns uncovered milk sour. His touch also blackens and rots potatoes which have been stored for the winter and dampens peats in the turf stacks so that they will not light when set on fire.

In some parts of Ireland, including Limerick and Cork, the Far Liath is believed to spread communal disease and sicknesses which he reputedly carries in the folds of his cloak. Colds, sore throats and influenza are all associated with him.

Grey Man

This fairy lacks the gift of speech and ignores the supplications of lost mariners and wayfarers. However, the phrase "God bless you!" appears to exert some power over him and may drive him away, at least for a while. A crucifix or holy medal, especially one which has been blessed by a bishop, may have a similar effect, but it should be remembered that such artefacts will not hold him at bay for very long. After this he will return, more virulent than ever. This did not prevent mariners long ago from setting medals into the prows of their boats, or country folk from leaving crucifixes among their turf piles to ward away evil. These were common practices until quite recently in certain rural areas.

"I had gathered all the potatoes in one year, just before the dark nights arrived," reports Johnny Aherne, a farmer from County Limerick. "I thought that they would be safe enough locked away in an outhouse at the back of my place. My father has warned me about the Far Liath, but to tell you the truth, I didn't pay him much heed. So, I piled the potatoes in the house and didn't bother to put any protections around them. They say that medals or holy water sprinkled about a place will keep the Far Liath away but I had no time for that. But the next morning I went to the outhouse and looked at the potatoes, and every one of them was black and not fit for eating. The Far Liath had touched them and he hadn't missed a single potato. Well, you may be sure that I always paid great attention to the old ways after that!"

Indeed, so much is he feared in certain areas that special paths are set aside for him to travel from place to place without interfering with humans. At Fair Head in north Antrim, a rock bridge is known locally as the Grey Man's Path and the Far Liath uses this regularly. Merely to glimpse him on his travels is to invite misfortune.

Land sheerie are found all
over Ireland, from Cork
to Donegal.

The Sheerie

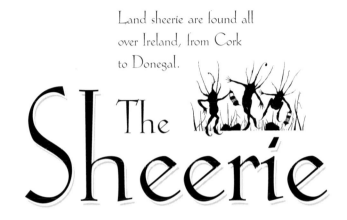

Variants:

tein sidhe

tein sionnic

Seán na gealaige

Liam na Lasoige

In some counties, they are considered
to be infallible harbingers of ill omen,
their very presence portending ill luck
and even death to anyone who sees
them. Their source of amusement is,
by sorcery, to lead astray those who
venture out after dark and cause them
to wander aimlessly all over the
countryside until the sheerie choose to
release them from the spell.

 # The Sheerie

"There was a big standing stone near the Mile Bridge, which I had to pass on my way home every evening. This time it was all lit up with dancing lights going backwards and forwards all around it. I knew that it was sheeries and was badly afraid but by good luck, I had an old iron horseshoe nail on me. I held it up and they let me pass without dragging me astray or taking my wits. But I never went back that way again."

The sheerie is one of the most unusual and potentially the most dangerous of all Irish fairies. Sheerie (the noun is both singular and collective) are strange, phosphorescent creatures who combine elements of both human and fairy nature. In most reports, they are little more than floating glimmers of light, observed around twilight, which move from cover to cover.

They are believed to be the souls of unbaptised children (probably those who died at birth) trying to return to the mortal world. In the meantime, they have become imbued with dark fairy magic, making them hostile towards humans. Indeed, it appears that their sole purpose is to cause misfortune to the living, of whom they are intensely jealous and to rejoice in any calamity which befalls humankind.

Sheerie are divided into two categories: water sheerie, which frequent marshy and coastal areas, and land sheerie, which lurk near the ruins of abandoned buildings such as farmhouses or mills.

Land sheerie are also seen in places associated with pagan tradition – raths, mounds and tumulae – and tend to be most active during the periods of the great pre-Christian festivals such as Bealtaine (30 April) or Samhain (31 October). Neither form of sheerie has the power of speech although they may emit a shrill, high pitched sound resembling that of blood singing in the ear. When heard continuously, it may even derange the human listener.

Accounts of both types of sheerie describe them as tiny, elf-like beings, with the faces of small children. One sighting, in County Mayo, describes them gathering over the waters of a treacherous bog:

"They were wee things, about the size of a full grown hare or a day old baby. They had a bit of brightness about them but it wasn't really a good light – more the sort of dull sheen that you'd get from dead things. A corpse-light, we call it. And there were some of them that seemed to be carrying wee lanterns and some were holding up bits of branches that looked to be burning at one end. And the air was full of their cries – wee, sharp sounds like a ringing in my ears. I couldn't describe it to you but you wouldn't mistake it for any other sound except maybe for snipe drumming (calling) out in the rushes. They were skipping and leaping all over the surface of the bog, at its most dangerous place."

Some people dismiss the sheerie as nothing more than
burning marsh gas, but against this explanation it has to
be pointed out that gases do not catch fire of their own
accord, nor do they flit about of their own volition.
As the old prayer from Connemara goes: "From ghosts,
sprites and the sheerie kind, Oh Lord protect us".

Water sheerie have acquired a particularly black reputation as a result of claims that they lure travellers to death or disaster in boggy or dangerous countryside. They do this by creating the illusion of a welcoming and well-lit dwelling in the distance. The sheerie light is actually hovering above a dark bog-hole into which the poor traveller may plunge and drown. Water sheerie are also known as 'corpse candles' because whoever follows them may quickly become a corpse.

Land sheerie are found all over Ireland, from Cork to Donegal. In some counties, they are considered to be infallible harbingers of ill omen, their very presence portending ill luck and even death to anyone who sees them. Their source of amusement is, by sorcery, to lead astray those who venture out after dark and cause them to wander aimlessly all over the countryside until the sheerie choose to release them from the spell.

Both water and land sheerie also have the power to temporarily derange any human they encounter. Surrounded by flitting and dazzling lights, perhaps lost and alone on dangerous ground, the traveller becomes increasingly confused and hysterical and may run backward and forward irrationally and speak senseless phrases. In this, the sheerie takes a special delight.

In some parts of Clare and Galway, both land and water sheerie appear not as radiant beings but as dark goblins. Travellers may be approached by a little man with a long, grey beard, clad in a black dress coat and holding a perpetually burning length of straw before him as a torch. He will beckon, as if to show the way to a welcoming inn, or to suggest that he knows a place where money is hidden. Those who follow, however, are invariably led into danger.
One way in which a sheerie can be warded off is by confronting it with a crucifix or iron implement. An alternative method is to turn your coat inside out and to recite the Paternoster prayer very loudly. Holy water will also drive them away but only for a short time.

It appears that fairy women
all over Ireland find birth a
difficult experience. Many
fairy children die before birth
and those that do survive,
are often stunted or
deformed creatures.

Changelings

Variants:
stocks

The adult fairies, who are aesthetic
beings, are repelled by these infants and
have no wish to keep them. They will try
to swap them with healthy children who
they steal from the mortal world. The
wizened, ill tempered creature left in
place of the human child is generally
known as a *changeling* and possesses the
power to work evil in a household. Any
child who is not baptised or who is
overly admired is especially at risk of
being exchanged.

Changelings

It is their temperament, however, which most marks the changeling. Babies are generally joyful and pleasant, but the fairy substitute is never happy, except when some calamity befalls the household. For the most part, it howls and screeches throughout its waking hours and the sound and frequency of its yells often transcend the bounds of mortal endurance.

A changeling can be one of three types: actual fairy children; senile fairies who are disguised as children; or, inanimate objects, such as pieces of wood which take on the appearance of a child through fairy magic. This latter type is known as a stock.

Puckered and wizened features coupled with yellow, parchment-like skin are all generic changeling attributes. This fairy will also exhibit very dark eyes, which betray a wisdom far older than its apparent years. Changelings display other characteristics, usually physical deformities, among which a crooked back or lame hand are common. About two weeks after their arrival in the human household, changelings will also exhibit a full set of teeth, legs as thin as chicken bones and hands which are curved and crooked as birds' talons and covered with a light, downy hair.

Changelings

No luck will come to a family in which there is a changeling because the creature drains away all the good fortune which would normally attend the household. Thus, those who are cursed with it tend to be very poor and struggle desperately to maintain the ravenous monster in their midst.

One positive feature which this fairy may demonstrate is an aptitude for music. As it begins to grow, the changeling may take up an instrument, often the fiddle or the Irish pipes, and plays with such skill that all who hear it will be entranced. This report is from near Boho in County Fermanagh:

"I saw a changeling one time. He lived with two oul' brothers away beyond the Dog's Well and looked like a wee wizened monkey. He was about ten or eleven but he couldn't really walk, just bobbed about. But he could play the whistle the best that you ever heard. Old tunes that the people has long forgotten, that was all he played. Then one day, he was gone and I don't know what happened to him at all".

Prevention being better than cure, a number of protections
may be placed around an infant's cradle to ward off a
changeling. A holy crucifix or iron tongs placed across the
cradle will usually be effective, because fairies fear these.
An article of the father's clothing laid across the child as
it sleeps will have the same effect.

Changelings

Changelings have prodigious appetites and will eat all that is set before them. The changeling has teeth and claws and does not take the breast like a human infant, but eats food from the larder. When the creature is finished each meal, it will demand more. Changelings have been known to eat the cupboard bare and still not be satisfied. Yet no matter how much it devours, the changeling remains as scrawny as ever.

Changelings do not live long in the mortal world. They usually shrivel up and die within the first two or three years of their human existence. The changeling is mourned and buried, but if its grave is ever disturbed all that will be found is a blackened twig or a piece of bog oak where the body of the infant should be. Some live longer but rarely into their teens.

There can also be adult changelings. These fairy doubles will exactly resemble the person taken but will have a sour disposition. The double will be cold and aloof and take no interest in friends or family, it will also be argumentative and scolding. As with an infant, a marked personality change is a strong indication of an adult changeling.

Changelings may be driven from a house. When this is achieved, the human child or adult will invariably be returned unharmed.

The least severe method of expulsion is to trick the fairy into revealing its true age. Another method is to force tea made from lusmore (foxglove) down the throat of a suspected changeling, burning out its human entrails and forcing it to flee back to the fairy realm. Heat and fire are anathema to the changeling and it will fly away.

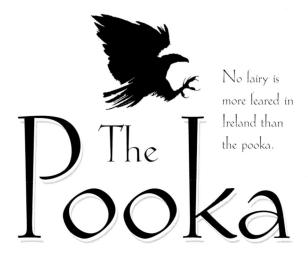

No fairy is
more feared in
Ireland than
the pooka.

The Pooka

Variants:

phouka

puca

This may be because it is always
out and about after nightfall,
creating harm and mischief, and
because it can assume a variety of
terrifying forms.

The Pooka

The guise in which it most often appears, however, it that of a sleek, dark horse with sulphurous yellow eyes and a long wild mane. In this form, it roams large areas of countryside at night, tearing down fences and gates, scattering livestock in terror, trampling crops and generally doing damage around remote farms.

In remote areas of County Down, the pooka becomes a small, deformed goblin who demands a share of the crop at the end of the harvest: for this reason several strands, known as the 'pooka's share', are left behind by the reapers. In parts of County Laois, the pooka becomes a huge, hairy bogeyman who terrifies those abroad at night; in Waterford and Wexford, it appears as an eagle with a massive wingspan; and in Roscommon, as a black goat with curling horns.

The mere sight of it may prevent hens laying their eggs or cows giving milk, and it is the curse of all late night travellers as it is known to swoop them up onto its back and then throw them into muddy ditches or bogholes. The pooka has the power of human speech, and it has been known to stop in front of certain houses and call out the names of those it wants to take upon its midnight dashes. If that person refuses, the pooka will vandalise their property because it is a very vindictive fairy.

The Pooka

The origins of the pooka are to some extent speculative. The name may come from the Scandinavian *pook* or *puke*, meaning 'nature spirit'. Such beings were very capricious and had to be continually placated or they would create havoc in the countryside, destroying crops and causing illness among livestock. Alternatively, the horse cults prevalent throughout the early Celtic world may have provided the underlying motif for the nightmare steed.

Other authorities suggest that the name comes from the early Irish *poc* meaning either 'a male goat' or 'a blow from a cudgel'. However, the horse cult origin is perhaps the most plausible since many of these cults met on high ground and the main abode of the pooka is believed to be on high mountain tops. There is a waterfall formed by the river Liffey in the Wicklow mountains known as the *Poula Phouk* (the pooka's hole), and Binlaughlin Mountain in County Fermanagh is also known as the 'peak of the speaking horse'.

The Pooka

In some areas of the country, the pooka is rather more mysterious than dangerous, provided it is treated with proper respect. The pooka may even be helpful on occasion, issuing prophesies and warnings where appropriate. For example the folklorist Douglas Hyde referred to a 'plump, sleek, terrible steed' which emerged from a hill in Leinster and which spoke in a human voice to the people there on the first day of November. It was accustomed to give "intelligent and proper answers to those who consulted it concerning all that would befall them until November the next year. And the people used to leave gifts and presents at the hill..."

Something similar seems to have occurred in south Fermanagh, where the tradition of gathering on certain high places to await a speaking horse was observed on Bilberry Sunday until quite recently.

Only one man has ever managed to ride the pooka and that was Brian Boru, the High King of Ireland. Using a special bridle containing three hairs from the pooka's tail, Brian managed to control the magic horse and stay on its back until, exhausted, it surrendered to his will. The king then extracted two promises from it; firstly, that it would no longer torment Christian people and ruin their property and secondly, that it would never again attack an Irishman (all other nationalities are exempt) except those who are drunk or abroad with an evil intent. The latter it could attack with greater ferocity than before. The pooka agreed to these conditions. However, over the intervening years, it seems to have forgotten its bargain and attacks on property and sober travellers on their way home continue to this day.

In most parts of the world, merrows take the form of a woman from the waist up and the form of a fish from the waist down.

Merrows

Variants:
silkies
mermaids

In Ireland, however, the only physical differences between merrows and humans are that the merrow's feet are flatter than those of a mortal and their hands have a thin webbing between the fingers.

Merrows

The word 'merrow' or *moruadh*, comes from the Irish *muir* (meaning sea) and *oigh* (meaning maid) and refers specifically to the female of the species.

Merfolk are also known as 'suire' which has been corrupted into the Scottish variant, silkie. While they undoubtedly exist, mermen — the merrows' male counterparts — have been rarely seen. The few descriptions that we have refer to them as being exceptionally ugly and scaled, with pig-like features and long, pointed teeth. Merrows themselves are extremely beautiful and perhaps not surprisingly given their disagreeable partners, are promiscuous in their relations with mortals.

The merrows, naturally enough, will also have a special affinity for water which humans do not share. Irish merrows are the fairy inhabitants of Tir fo Thoinn (the Land beneath the Waves), a vast undersea continent, although they are amphibious and can also live on land for long periods.

Many coastal dwellers have taken merrows as lovers and a number of famous Irish families claim their descent from such unions, notably the O'Flaherty and O'Sullivan families of Kerry and the MacNamaras of Clare. The Irish poet W B Yeats reported a further case in his *Irish Fairy and Folk Tales*: "Near Bantry in the last century, there is said to have been a woman, covered in scales like a fish, who was descended from such a marriage".

Merrows have special clothing to enable them to travel through ocean currents. In Kerry, Cork and Wexford, they wear a small red cap made from feathers, called a *cohullen druith*.

However, in more northerly waters they travel through the sea wrapped in sealskin cloaks and take on the appearance and attributes of seals. In order to come ashore, the merrow must abandon her cap or cloak, so any mortal who finds these has power over her, as she cannot return to the sea until they are retrieved.

Bargains between sea-folk and mortals regarding these items are commonplace around the Irish coast. There are numerous instances of fishermen hiding the cloaks in the thatches of their house and then persuading the merrow to marry them. In each case, the merrow eventually finds the cloak and her urge to return to the sea is so strong that she leaves her human husband and children behind and returns there.

It should be noted that although the merrow makes an excellent wife and is a good cook, a married sea-woman rarely laughs or shows affection to either her husband or children. Moreover, merrow brides are often extremely wealthy, with fortunes of gold which their kind has plundered from shipwrecks. Consequently, marriage with one of the sea-people can establish a man for life if he can put up with a partner who is cold and aloof.

Some so-called merrows are not sea-people at all, but have human origins. These are usually children involved in some nautical disaster who have been carried away and raised by the merfolk in Tir fo Thoinn. They tend to forget their human origins and to live quite happily among the sea-people. If they set foot on land again however, their human memories return and they can no longer return to the sea.

Merrows

One such was St Murgen, a holy woman who lived in the north of
Ireland during the sixth century. Originally a human girl named Liban,
she lived with her parents on the coast of Scotland. During a storm,
her parents were drowned and she was carried away by a severe
flood. Many years later (the given date is 588) she was caught in nets
placed across Belfast Lough. In the intervening period, she had lived
with merrows under the sea. She later changed her name to Murgen,
accepted Christianity and performed many healing miracles
throughout Ireland. When she died she was buried in St Cuthbert's
church at Dunluce in north Antrim, where a seashell motif on her
tomb still marks her years amongst the merfolk.

It should not be assumed that merrows are kindly and well-disposed
towards mortals. As members of the *sidhe*, or Irish fairy world, they
have a natural antipathy towards humans. Merrows will only marry
humans so that their children have a chance of reaching heaven by
virtue of having human blood in their veins. It is therefore unwise to
fall asleep close to the seashore without some form or protection,
such as a crucifix or medallion, in case the sea-folk attempt to drown
the sleeper by dragging him under the waves. Moreover, if you have to
sleep on a beach then it is advisable to sleep within the sound of a
church bell, since the sound will drive away the malignant sea-folk.
No merrow will enter a church, so it is also reasonable to assume
safety within its precincts from her attentions.

In some parts of Ireland, merrows are regarded as messengers of
doom and death and it is thought to be especially unlucky to see one.
Fishermen in Kerry, for example, will turn back to port if they see a
merrow sitting upon a rock. There are also reports of a particular
merrow who sits combing her long hair on a rocky island in the
middle of the River Shannon. Those who see her will reputedly die
within one year. Despite her wealth and beauty, you should be
particularly wary about encountering this marine fairy.

Folklorists debate whether the banshee is a fairy, spirit or mortal.

The Banshee

Variants:
bean=nighe
bean=chaointe

Her Irish name, *bean-sidhe* (woman of the fairy), suggests that she is of the fairy race but some view her as a vengeful ghost who will follow a family which has done her harm and will take delight in the deaths of its members. Others have described her as an ancestral spirit whom God has appointed to forewarn members of certain ancient Irish families of their time of death.

The Banshee

One of the best known supernatural figures in Ireland is the banshee, the restless spirit which follows those Irish families with pure Celtic blood in their veins and warns them of death with her wailing keen.

In 1437, King James I of Scotland was approached by an Irish 'seeress' or banshee who foretold his murder at the instigation of the Earl of Atholl. This is an example of the banshee in human form. There are records of several human banshees or prophetesses attending the great houses of Ireland and the courts of local Irish kings.

Whatever her origins, the banshee chiefly appears in one of three guises: a young woman, a stately matron or a raddled old hag. These represent the triple aspects of the Celtic goddess of war and death, namely Badhbh, Macha and Mor-Rioghain. She usually wears either a grey, hooded cloak or the winding sheet or grave robe of the unshriven dead. She may also appear as a washer-woman, and is seen apparently washing the blood-stained clothes of those who are about to die. In this guise she is known as the *bean-nighe* (washing woman).

She has also appeared in a variety of other forms, such as that of a hooded crow, stoat, hare and weasel. All these animals are associated in Ireland with witchcraft and give the banshee a sinister magical aspect.

However, it is for signalling death through the Irish keen that the banshee is best known.

The Banshee

Although not always seen, her mourning call is heard, usually at night when someone is about to die. In some parts of Leinster, she is referred to as the *bean chaointe* (keening woman) whose wail can be so piercing that it shatters glass. In Kerry, the keen is experienced as a "low, pleasant singing"; in Tyrone as "the sound of two boards being struck together"; and on Rathlin Island as "a thin, screeching sound, somewhere between the wail of a woman and the moan of an owl".

There is some dispute as to whether the banshee only cries for the dying members of the old aristocratic families of Ireland or whether she cries for all expiring Irishmen. According to tradition, the banshee can only cry for five major Irish families – the O'Neills, the O'Briens, the O'Connors, the O'Gradys and the Kavanaghs – since these were the only true Gaelic families without Norman blood in their veins. However, from the twelfth century onwards, these families began to intermarry with incoming English settlers, forming new families and clans, and the banshee began to extend her attention to these as well. Unlike other Irish fairies, water appears to be no barrier to her, since she will cry for her charges no matter where in the world they may be. Reports cite the banshee being heard in such diverse places as Canada and Australia, almost anywhere Irish immigrants have settled in number.

Those who attempt to catch the banshee have a difficult task because she travels very quickly. In Clare and Galway, she reputedly "glides quicker than human feet can walk", while in Mayo she appears to "hop like a magpie and even a horse at full stretch can't overtake her".

The Banshee

A number of descriptions of the banshee have been recorded over the years. She is usually seen as a face at a window or glimpsed from a distance. In some cases, she is either washing or combing her hair, or beetling clothes. On no account should she be approached, for great misfortune will befall those who do and this will pass down through generations. The experiences of one Thomas Reilly of Galway who tried to catch the banshee, should serve as a warning: he died within seconds of the incident and his son Michael inherited the family farm, which never prospered. Michael had four children, all of whom were feeble minded. He himself took cancer which ate away at his face and killed him. Others too have tried to steal the banshee's comb or her beetle and have suffered similar fates.

Perhaps the most famous banshee was Aoibheall, who appeared to the Irish chieftain Dunlang O'Hartigan on 23 April 1014, just before the Battle of Clontarf. She begged him not to take part in the battle, promising him life and happiness for two hundred years if he would refrain from fighting for a single day. O'Hartigan, the foremost of Brian Boru's lieutenants, stoutly refused. Aoibheall then foretold the victory of the Irish troops but also prophesied that O'Hartigan and his son Turlough, together with Brian Boru, would all perish in the battle. The prophesy came true, and Aoibheall was seen keening loudly for the fallen Irish as the sun went down over the battlefield. She went on to become the banshee or seeress of the Royal House of Munster and may still be seen and heard on the heights above Lough Derg.

Although the leprechaun has been described as Ireland's national fairy, this name was originally only used in the north Leinster area.

The Leprechaun

Variants:
lurachmain
lurican
lurgadhan

In Ulster, the term for this fairy was *lurachmain*, in Connaught *lurican* and in Munster *lurgadhan*. Today, the north Leinster name is widely accepted in all parts of Ireland.

Leprechauns take the form of aged, diminutive men who usually function as fairy shoemakers. Indeed, the name leprechaun may have derived from the Irish *leith bhrogan* (shoemaker), although it has also been suggested that its origins may lie in *luacharma'n* (Irish for pygmy).

The Leprechaun

Leprechauns are usually described as small, untidy men, about three feet in height, dressed in green coats with red breeches buckled at the knee, woollen stockings and wide-brimmed hats slightly askew at one side. They constantly smoke foul smelling pipes, called dudeens and tend to have a surly and sour disposition.

Not surprisingly, the leprechaun is a solitary creature and is to be found inhabiting sheughs (gullys) or lurking behind bushes or under hedges. Tapping on a shoe that he is making, the sound of his labour is the only signal that he is there.

They are frequently to be found in an intoxicated state, caused by the consumption of poteen which they brew themselves. However, they never become so drunk that the hand which holds the hammer becomes unsteady and their work affected. If anything, too much drink makes them even more sullen and argumentative.

Female leprechauns do not appear to exist and there is much speculation as to how these fairies actually reproduce. Leprechauns themselves are extremely secretive about their origins but it is believed that they may be the offspring of unions between mortals and fairies who have been cast out of their respective worlds.

Leprechauns carry two leather pouches. In one there is a silver shilling, a magical coin that returns to the purse each time it is paid out so that the leprechaun appears to be paying out money without ever actually losing any. In the other he carries a gold coin which he uses to try and bribe his way out of difficult situations. This coin usually turns to leaves or ashes once the leprechaun has parted with it.

From this, it may be deduced that the leprechaun can be capricious. He has to be because in addition to his trade as a cobbler, he is the banker of the fairy world. Leprechauns know where large caches of ancient wealth are hidden and have become self-appointed guardians of this wealth. Other fairies must go to the leprechaun when they want gold for their revelries or for fairy largesse. The leprechaun's sullen disposition would shame even the most insensitive bank-manager. Leprechauns have collected much of the ancient treasure left by the Danes when they marauded through Ireland and have buried it in crocks or pots. The leprechaun has a phenomenal memory and knows the exact location of each crock and can easily recover it, if he wishes. However, most leprechauns are natural misers and will not easily part with their money.

Leprechauns tend to avoid contact with humans. They do this because they regard them as foolish, flighty creatures and also because they fear that humans may steal the treasures which they so carefully guard. Moreover, despite their squat and stocky build, the leprechaun is incredibly sprightly and can move quicker than the human eye can see. Most humans only catch a fleeting glimpse as he skips out of their line of vision behind a tree or under a bush. If caught by a mortal, he will promise great wealth if allowed to go free. However, you must never take your eye off him, for he can vanish in an instant, leaving the watcher astonished at his alacrity.

So, his sour disposition and natural aversion to humans does not prevent the leprechaun from rewarding those whom he believes have done him a good turn. He has a strong sense of honour and will always return one good deed for another. Unfortunately, such rewards tend to take the form of strong liquor which invariably leaves the recipient very much the worse for wear.

The Leprechaun

It would appear that the leprechaun family is split into two distinct groups. There is much debate as to whether the cluricaun is actually a type of leprechaun or a degenerate close cousin. Certainly there is a physical resemblance between the two fairy types, although each has quite a different temperament. The leprechaun is industrious but sullen, the cluricaun is indolent and cheery. While the leprechaun wears green, the cluricaun likes to dress up and wear garish colours. In fact, he sometimes resembles a down-at-heel country gentleman out on a spree.

Unlike leprechauns, cluricauns never carry money nor do they have any knowledge of hidden hoards of gold, usually stealing what they want instead of buying it. Like their wealthier counterparts, they are partial to strong drink and will unashamedly raid the wine cellars and cocktail cabinets of the rich, draining all casks and bottles there. They will also enter larders at night and eat all they can before morning because they have prodigious appetites. For their own amusement, they will create mayhem in a house during the hours of darkness, overturning chairs, breaking plates or hiding things so that they cannot be found.

Cluricauns will also harness sheep, goats, dogs, even domestic fowl and ride them throughout the country at night. They will break down fences and walls, and chase cattle all over the countryside, giving additional work to the poor farmer. Then, from under a hedge and with a jug of stolen poteen at their side, the cluricauns will laugh at foolish mortals as they try to repair the damage done.

Leprechauns formally disapprove of such unseemly behaviour and disassociate themselves from the cluricaun's activities. There are some who wonder if the cluricaun is not simply a leprechaun indulging in drunken revelry...

The dullahan is one of the most
spectacular creatures in the Irish fairy
realm and one which is particularly
active in the more remote parts of counties
Sligo and Down.

The Dullahan

Variants:
dullaghan
far dorocha
Crom Dubh

Around midnight on certain Irish
festivals or feast days, this wild and
black-robed horseman may be
observed riding a dark and snorting
steed across the countryside.

The Dullahan

W J Fitzpatrick, a storyteller
from the Mourne Mountains in
County Down, recounts :

"I seen the dullahan myself, stopping on the brow of the hill between Bryansford and Moneyscalp late one evening, just as the sun was setting. It was completely headless but it held up its own head in its hand and I heard it call out a name. I put my hands across my ears in case the name was my own, so I wouldn't hear what it said. When I looked again, it was gone. But shortly afterwards, there was a bad car accident on that very hill and a young man was killed. It had been his name that the dullahan was calling".

Dullahans are headless. Although the dullahan has no head upon its shoulders, he carries it with him, either on the saddle-brow of his horse or upraised in his right hand. The head is the colour and texture of stale dough or mouldy cheese, and quite smooth. A hideous, idiotic grin splits the face from ear to ear, and the eyes, which are small and black, dart about like malignant flies. The entire head glows with the phosphorescence of decaying matter and the creature may use it as a lantern to guide its way along the darkened laneways of the Irish countryside. Wherever the dullahan stops, a mortal dies.

The dullahan is possessed of supernatural sight. By holding his severed head aloft, he can see for vast distances across the countryside, even on the darkest night. Using this power, he can spy the house of a dying person, no matter where it lies. Those who watch from their windows to see him pass are rewarded for their pains by having a basin of blood thrown in their faces, or by being struck blind in one eye.

The Dullahan

The dullahan is usually mounted on a black steed, which thunders through the night. He uses a human spine as a whip. The horse sends out sparks and flames from its nostrils as it charges forth. In some parts of the country, such as County Tyrone, the dullahan drives a black coach known as the coach-a-bower (from the Irish *coiste bodhar*, meaning 'deaf or silent coach'). This is drawn by six black horses, and travels so fast that the friction created by its movement often sets on fire the bushes along the sides of the road. All gates fly open to let rider and coach through, no matter how firmly they are locked, so no one is truly safe from the attentions of this fairy.

This fairy has a limited power of speech. Its disembodied head is permitted to speak just once on each journey it undertakes, and then has only the ability to call the name of the person whose death it heralds. A dullahan will stop its snorting horse before the door of a house and shout the name of the person about to die, drawing forth the soul at the call. He may also stop at the very spot where a person will die.

On nights of Irish feast days, it is advisable to stay at home with the curtains drawn; particularly around the end of August or early September when the festival of Crom Dubh reputedly took place. If you have to be abroad at this time, be sure to keep some gold object close to hand.

The Dullahan

The origins of the dullahan are not known for certain, but he is thought to be the embodiment of an ancient Celtic god, Crom Dubh, or Black Crom. Crom Dubh was worshipped by the prehistoric king, Tighermas, who ruled in Ireland about fifteen hundred years ago and who legitimised human sacrifice to heathen idols. Being a fertility god, Crom Dubh demanded human lives each year, the most favoured method of sacrifice being decapitation. The worship of Crom continued in Ireland until the sixth century, when Christian missionaries arrived from Scotland. They denounced all such worship and under their influence, the old sacrificial religions of Ireland began to lose favour. Nonetheless, Crom Dubh was not to be denied his annual quota of souls, and took on a physical form which became known as the *dullahan* or *far dorocha* (meaning dark man), the tangible embodiment of death.

Unlike the banshee, the dullahan does not pursue specific families and its call is a summoning of the soul of a dying person rather than a death warning. There is no real defence against the dullahan because he is death's herald. However, an artefact made of gold may frighten him away, for dullahans appear to have an irrational fear of this precious metal. Even a small amount of gold may suffice to drive them off, as the following account from County Galway relates:

"A man was on his way home one night between Roundstone and Ballyconneely. It was just getting dark and, all of a sudden, he heard the sound of horse's hooves pounding along the road behind him. Looking around, he saw the dullahan on his charger, hurtling towards him at a fair speed. With a loud shout, he made to run but the thing came on after him, gaining on him all the time. In truth, it would have overtaken him and carried him away had he not dropped a gold-headed pin from the folds of his shirt on the road behind him. There was a roar in the air above him and, when he looked again, the dullahan was gone".

Some Lesser Known

Irish Fairies

Butter Spirit

Butter spirits usually appear in the guise of little old men, dressed in green and usually no more than one or two feet high. Found all over Ireland but mainly in Counties Sligo and Monaghan, they are distantly related to the *leprechaun* but are much more roguish and thieving in their ways. They will steal things which are not fastened down and will take food which is not marked with the sign of the Cross. They particularly enjoy fresh butter and will draw off the "good" of the milk before it is churned. All that will remain is an unusable froth which will not yield any butter at all. Some sources state that they will never take "from the poor man's table" but steal only from the rich. They are to be seen at night with their lanterns to light their way and their grappling hooks for climbing into inaccessible places or onto high shelves, always on the look-out for something to steal. These fairies are also known in England where their favourite haunts are rich abbeys where the monks have grown self-indulgent and idle – for this reason the English variants are sometimes known as *abbey lubbers*.

Skeaghshee or Oakshee

The *skeaghshee* are primarily tree spirits, *skeagh* meaning an isolated tree; *shee* or *sidhe* meaning fairy, which are given guardianship of particular growths. All over Ireland, it is widely regarded as taboo to cut down a "fairy tree" and it is the function of the skeaghshee to ensure that those who are unwise enough to do so suffer retribution. Skeaghshee are to be found everywhere in Ireland, wherever there are lonely trees or bushes. Their powers are unlimited – they can inflict disease, insanity, poverty or bad-luck on anyone who violates the fairy tree over which they have jurisdiction – and these powers can even bring misfortune to the family of that person if the skeaghshee is so inclined. These are certainly not fairies to be trifled with and so before tampering with the landscape, it is advisable to check if there is a fairy tree in your way.

Far Darrig

The *far* or *fir darrig*, properly specific to Donegal although mentioned elsewhere as well, is a somewhat elusive character. No proper description of him actually exists and his name "The Red Man" gives no real clue as to what he looks like. Even his height is a matter of dispute – some authorities class him as a "small person in a red coat" whilst others portray him as a grey giant. He is a trickster and will play terrible and sometimes gruesome pranks on unsuspecting mortals. Aside from this, he often shows up at a person's door on a cold night and demands to be let in to the fire. It is unwise to refuse him because if he is driven away, he will take "the luck of the house" with him. The far darrig is not noted for personal hygiene and many householders may have to put up with his rather unpleasant smell for many days after his departure.

Watershee

Perhaps one of the most deceiving of all fairies is the *watershee*.
Mostly female, this fairy is found in many marshy areas such as the
Bog of Allen and corresponds to our stylised image of the fairy –
small, delicate and gossamer-winged. At other times, she appears as
a beautiful woman. Appearances of course can be deceptive for
this is an extremely deadly spirit. Like the *sheerie*, the watershee
will lure travellers into bogs and lakes through her innocent
appearance or sweet singing. There she will drown them and,
reputedly, devour their soul. Only the wearing of a Cross or other
holy amulet or the saying of a prayer
will protect humans from her dark
and evil ways.